MW00737351

TOMORROW'S CHILD

JOANNE SUTER

GLOBE FEARON
Pearson Learning Group

The PACEMAKER BESTELLERS

Bestellers I

Diamonds in the Dirt	Flight to Fear
Night of the Kachina	The Time Trap
The Verlaine Crossing	The Candy Man
Silvabamba	Three Mile House
The Money Game	Dream of the Dead

Bestellers II

Black Beach	The Demeter Star
Crash Dive	North to Oak Island
Wind Over Stonehenge	So Wild a Dream
Gypsy	Wet Fire
Escape from Tomorrow	Tiger, Lion, Hawk

Bestellers III

Star Gold	The Animals
Bad Moon	Counterfeit!
Jungle Jenny	Night of Fire and Blood
Secret Spy	Village of Vampires
Little Big Top	I Died Here

Bestellers IV

Dares	The Cardiff Hill Mystery
Welcome to Skull Canyon	Tomorrow's Child
Blackbeard's Medal	Hong Kong Heat
Time's Reach	Follow the Whales
Trouble at Catskill Creek	A Changed Man

Cover and interior illustrator: Sarah Waldron

ISBN 0-8224-5341-X

Printed in the United States of America

5 6 7 8 9   06 05 04 03 02   1-800-321-3106
                                               www.pearsonlearning.com

CONTENTS

CHAPTER **1**

WAKING

Kate Dial woke up at 4:51. The green numbers on the clock beside her bed gave the room its only light. Kate felt as if she were floating. She kept looking at the clock because she had turned toward it in her sleep. She did not feel strong enough to move her head.

The clock flashed 4:52. Then it showed the day: 5-12-2085. Kate closed her eyes. She tried to remember why she felt so tired.

Kate Dial was 24 years old. She was a 20–A. She'd gotten the "20" score because she was smart. It was the highest score possible. The "A" score came about thanks to Kate's fine body. A's were given to the best athletes. As a 20–A, Kate was both a genius and a great athlete. She had a good job as a chemist in the

1

Metro Chem Lab. And each year she took first place at the Inter-Metro Games.

Kate's husband, Josh, was a 20-A also. He was a top man in the Metro Transport Department. From time to time the government sent him on trips into the Wilds. Josh made maps of the lands outside the Metro.

Kate and Josh Dial were rich. They were young, good-looking, and in fine shape.

Fine shape! Kate thought. If that were so, what was she doing in the hospital?

Kate hadn't stayed in a hospital before. She'd grown up in a warm, loving youth camp right there in the Metro. Her parents, she was told, had died when she was just a baby. She never really knew much about them or how they had died. When no one answered her questions, Kate learned to stop asking.

Kate had been happy in the youth camp. There were many children there. Most of them were very bright, like herself.

Kate lived in the camp until she was 18. She met Josh there. It seemed they were often thrown together. Josh's parents, the records said, had left him when he was very young. Like Kate, Josh had learned not to question what the records said.

Kate found Josh to be kind, smart, and good-looking.

"I love you," Josh told Kate when they were just 16. "You're beautiful. We have such good times together. I think we're made for each other."

Two years after leaving the camp, Kate and Josh were married.

Now bits and pieces of her life with Josh floated through Kate's mind. She lay watching the clock. 5:30 A.M. May 12, 2085.

They both liked their jobs and their home, and they loved each other. Their life together had been grand. They lived on the 121st floor of a lovely building in the heart of the Metro. They were high enough above the fog bank to be able to see blue sky. The tops of neighboring buildings rose up out of the white fog. Most weather, which was carefully controlled, went on below them.

Josh and Kate had been very happy during the last year. The government had sent them off to map the Wilds. The two of them had gone out alone.

Kate had really liked the citizen camp and its small wooden buildings. In the camp, people who couldn't handle life in the Metro had come together to live. Kate and Josh had made friends in the camp, even though they might never see those friends again. Now, however, all that seemed like something that had happened a very long time ago. It seemed almost like a dream.

Kate remembered that she and Josh had been very excited about something then. But she couldn't recall what it was.

When the hospital clock read 6:00, Doctor Penn came in.

"Kate," she smiled, "you're looking fine this morning." She held up a mirror so Kate could look at herself. The doctor wasn't lying. Kate looked a little tired, perhaps, and a bit round and heavy. But for a sick person she still looked very pretty. Kate's soft blue hair lay against the white sheets. The dark blue hospital dress made her eyes seem bluer than ever. The glamour-expert had been right. Blue was Kate's color.

Kate felt better just thinking that if she looked okay, she probably was okay.

"I don't remember," she said to Dr. Penn. Her voice felt thick, as if she hadn't spoken in a long time. "Why am I here?"

Dr. Penn took Kate's hand. The doctor's touch was cool and dry.

"Don't worry, my dear," Dr. Penn said. "You're in good hands. You've had a little stomach problem. We had to go in and take out a small growth. But in a day or two, it will seem as if this had never happened."

"What *is* happening?" Kate asked Dr. Penn. "I can remember things from long ago, but I can't remember what went on just last week. I can't remember being sick or coming to the hospital."

"Don't you worry, dear," Dr. Penn said again. "That kind of thing often happens right after an operation. Soon everything will be just like it always was."

Kate smiled. She had learned as a child to believe what she was told. And now, like a child, she took Dr. Penn's word.

Dr. Penn smiled back at Kate. She smiled, but her eyes were cool and blank. The doctor wore a light green coat and pants. Her green hair was cut short. Green was such a nice cool color.

"Now, here we go," Dr. Penn said, taking Kate's arm. "I'm going to give you a little more Luradine."

Kate nodded. She knew that this drug the government passed out freely would help her rest. Kate looked forward to floating away from her worries.

Dr. Penn held the dose gun against Kate's arm. In a second Kate felt lighter.

Then there was a bright red flash behind her eyes and a pounding in her head. I've never heard of Luradine doing this, Kate thought. She was afraid. She tried to stop the pounding, but it was too strong. All the while she could hear Dr. Penn telling her something over and over. Kate couldn't understand the words.

She looked into the doctor's cool green eyes. Then the pounding stopped, and everything became dark.

CHAPTER 2

REMEMBERING

Kate spent much of the next five days sleeping. From time to time, Dr. Penn would come in to see her.

When her husband visited, Kate worried over him.

"You look so tired, Josh. Have you been sleeping? Don't worry about me. Please."

Josh didn't look well. Usually his skin was dark. Now it was very white against his black hair and black suit.

"I can't help worrying about you, Kate. The doctors have given me medicine to help me sleep. They have me on Luradine four times a day. And I'm seeing a rest-expert too."

Kate reached for Josh's hand. She was surprised to find that it was shaking. Josh was always so much in control, so sure of himself.

The doctor was still keeping Kate on heavy doses of drugs. The drugs kept her from thinking clearly. Remembering was hard work. It was always just before taking another dose that Kate could do it. The last dose would wear off, and her mind would clear. In the time before the doctor came in again, she could remember little things.

Kate thought about a room. It was a small room with light yellow walls. Kate did not know where the room was, but she knew it was freshly painted. She could almost smell the paint. The room was empty but for something that stood in the corner.

Kate fought to make the picture clearer. It was a tiny horse, a rocking horse that was standing in the corner.

Kate slept a lot during her time in the hospital. Sometimes she'd wake with a start. She was pulled from sleep by the high drawn out noise of a crying baby. But when Kate listened hard, all became still. There was no baby. There was no one crying.

Dr. Penn decided Kate could get out of bed. She walked the hospital halls, her legs shaking at first. The drug doses came less often, but they were still strong. They still brought on the flashing light and the strong pounding. There was always the sound of a doctor's voice saying something Kate could not understand. The doctor would say it over and over.

Kate questioned Dr. Penn about the drug.

"Take my word, Kate," Dr. Penn said. "It's only Luradine. I'm not sure why you're feeling it like you say you are. But look how strong you're getting. The drug is doing wonders for you. Trust me, my dear. Why, we wouldn't let anything happen to you. You mean a lot to us. Just trust me."

"Dr. Penn," Kate said, "I'm a chemist myself. I know how Luradine acts. This is very different."

Dr. Penn stopped smiling. "Mrs. Dial," she said. "Why are you questioning me? I *am* your doctor."

Kate backed down. She never questioned those in charge, just as no one questioned her work in Chem Lab.

Kate smiled to make things right again. "It's true, Dr. Penn," she said. "I am feeling better each day."

Dr. Penn smiled coolly and patted Kate's hand. Then she put the dose gun against Kate's

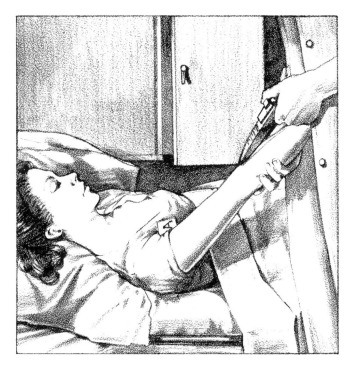

arm and looked into her eyes. The drug always worked quickly.

Slowly Kate's body grew stronger. There were still bandages on her stomach. And the stitches under the bandages hurt just a little. But she felt quite well. She could not, however, get a clear picture of the time before her operation. She could not remember going to the hospital.

"You were sick," was all Josh said. "You were sick, so I took you to the hospital. I was worried. The doctor said I was making myself sick worrying. She gave me medicine too. I'm still taking the medicine, and it helps. We're both just fine now." Josh smiled his wonderful smile and put his arms around Kate.

Josh went with Kate on her walks around the hospital halls. One day they walked a bit farther than they ever had before. They ended up in the birthing ward. Looking into the rooms there, they saw happy mothers holding little babies.

Kate's blue eyes opened wide. She stood still as stone. "Listen!" she said. "Just listen!"

"What is it?" Josh asked. "All I hear are crying babies."

Kate shook her head. She grabbed Josh's arm hard.

"It's for me, Josh," she whispered. "Somewhere a baby is crying for me."

CHAPTER 3

Kate Dial had a strong will. The doctor had not known just how strong it could be. Most people took the words of the experts and asked no questions. They did what they were told. Kate could no longer do this. Her mind would not rest, even when heavy with drugs. She lay awake at night feeling the bandages on her stomach. She tried to remember her operation but could not. And she still pictured the yellow room and heard a baby's cries.

When she left the hospital, Kate was sure she hadn't had the operation they said she'd had.

"Good-bye, Kate." Dr. Penn waved. "Don't forget, now. Three times a week you're coming in for your medicine. We'll be looking for you."

Outside the hospital, Josh opened the bubble top on their little metro-transport. He helped Kate in and pushed a button to join their car to the transport lines. The little machine rushed them home.

"Surprise!" Josh said to Kate when they were back in their own apartment. He showed her the newly decorated study.

"We need a place to work at home," he said. Then a funny look came over his face. "At least, I think we do. It was the doctor's idea. She said you'd be working at home until you're completely well."

Kate was, indeed, surprised. "It's beautiful, Josh," she said. "When did you have time to do it?"

"It was all done while I was at work," Josh answered. "All in one day. Dr. Penn took care of everything. She called in the painters, ordered the desk, the chairs. I didn't have to do a thing."

Josh still looks tired, Kate thought. Tired and different.

Suddenly she wanted to get out of the beautiful new study. The smell of the fresh paint was making her sick. And the smell of that paint caused a picture to flash in her mind. It was the yellow room again, a room just about the same size as their study.

But, even thinking hard, Kate could not remember any yellow room in their apartment. The extra room that was now their study had been painted a dark green. Now it was white. Kate remembered using it only as a place to store things.

Every day now Kate was bothered by flashes of strange thoughts. She saw the yellow room over and over again. She heard crying.

One night she woke from a very strong dream. The crying had seemed so real and so much like someone calling out to her.

Kate got up, being careful not to wake Josh. Like a sleepwalker, she slipped softly down the hall to the study.

She went into the study and sat in the big chair behind the desk. The study was quiet. Kate looked around the room. Then she turned in the chair and looked out the window at the night sky. There were red and blue lights on the tops of the other buildings. The white fog lay thick below.

Then Kate heard the crying again. From out in the dark, she heard a baby crying.

Kate went to the window. It filled one wall of the study. She pressed against it. There was nothing outside that she had not seen before.

She went back to the desk and turned on the desk lamp. Then she walked to the far corner of the room.

She bent down and ran her hand over the thick carpet. Kate could feel marks, places where the carpet had been pressed down. She looked closely. There were two lines in the carpet. A picture played in Kate's mind. There was a rocking horse standing in the corner of a room. Those lines she felt on the carpet could have been made by that rocking horse.

"Josh!" Kate called.

Josh came hurrying down the hall, pulling a black shirt over his head. He found Kate sitting on the floor in the corner. She was looking at her own stomach, fingering the front of her blue nightgown. Tears streamed down her face.

Kate reached out and took Josh's hand. She placed it on her stomach. Josh could feel the small bandage she still wore. Kate was shaking.

"What is it, Kate?" Josh asked. "What's the matter?"

"There was a baby, Josh," Kate cried. "I know it! They must have taken it from me. But Josh, we had a baby!"

CHAPTER **4**

THE DOCTOR'S VISIT

"The doctor told me this might happen, Kate. She said you might think all kinds of strange things for a time. It happens often after an operation like yours."

Josh held Kate close. He was very sweet, but he did not believe her. Kate began to wonder if she were right about the baby.

The days passed. Kate stayed at home. The Chem Lab sent her paper work, and Kate spent hours behind her new desk. Friends that Kate hadn't seen in a long time stopped by to visit.

She and Josh had been out exploring the Wilds for almost a year. Then she had gone right into the hospital. Most of her friends were surprised to hear about the operation. They were kind and brought flowers and presents.

Josh pressed Kate to get back to her old life. He asked people to dinner. The two of them watched shows together on the wall-screen. Some days Kate really believed everything was fine. Other days she heard the crying.

Kate wanted someone to explain things to her. She tried to remember what had happened. She thought about it so long and hard that her head hurt.

Maybe Josh was right, Kate thought. How could I have had a child and not remember it?

Yet Kate knew that drugs could do strange things. There were drugs that made minds weak and open to control. Kate had seen the power of such drugs in the Chem Lab. She also knew that there were top-secret chemicals that even she knew little about.

Kate was still supposed to go to the hospital three times a week. "Follow-up care," Dr. Penn called it. Kate got a dose of what they said was Luradine at each visit. Josh kept up his medicine too. He was sure that it helped him sleep.

It was Tuesday morning. The picture on the wall-screen showed a rainy day in the Metro. It had been dry too long, so Weather Control had planned two wet days.

Kate was getting ready to leave the apartment. It was time for her visit to Dr. Penn. She looked in the mirror at the dark circles under her eyes. Her makeup would not hide them. Kate had been wakened many times last night by that sound that only she could hear.

"Go back to sleep," Josh had mumbled. "I don't hear anything."

It was hard to wake Josh when he had taken his pills. And though he slept and slept, he still seemed tired.

"I'm not going to go!" Kate said out loud to the empty apartment. "I don't need any more drugs. I'm not going to see Dr. Penn."

What would happen, Kate wondered, if she did not take her medicine? What might she remember?

It did not take long for Dr. Penn to come looking for Kate. She showed up at Kate's door later the same day.

"Don't be fooled, Kate," the doctor said. "You aren't well yet." Her face was serious under her green hat. "It isn't smart to miss your medicine."

"I'm taking myself off all drugs," Kate said. She could hardly believe that she was speaking out like this. "I'm feeling fine!"

"It's a bad idea," Dr. Penn said. "A very bad idea. We know what's best for our people." Dr. Penn locked her green eyes into Kate's blue ones.

Kate knew about mind-bending. She knew that a person's thoughts could be changed. The drugs she'd been taking had made her an easy subject. Kate felt her will breaking down as Dr. Penn looked into her eyes.

Kate tried to look away but could not. Dr. Penn took the dose gun out of her green bag. She then rolled up the arm of Kate's blue shirt. The drug rocked Kate's mind.

It's more than Luradine, Kate thought as Dr. Penn helped her into a chair. It's much more.

The doctor stood behind Kate now, rubbing the sides of Kate's head with her fingers. "Just rest," she said. "You'll be able to go on with your work in an hour or so."

Dr. Penn kept on lightly rubbing Kate's head. "You must not question me, dear. You must listen to me and believe me. I am right. I am right about yesterday and about today and about tomorrow."

Dr. Penn put the dose gun back in her bag. "And Kate," she said.

Kate looked at the doctor through half-closed eyes.

"Don't forget your Thursday visit. We don't want to have to put you back in the hospital."

Kate wasn't able to think again until Wednesday. She felt like the robot that did the jobs around the house. Kate ate breakfast, lunch, and dinner. She smiled at her husband.

She watched the wall-screen. It was almost time for her next visit to the doctor before she started remembering. Now the baby's cries were harder to hear. They sounded far, far away. The picture of the yellow room had become dim.

It's going, Kate thought. It's all slipping away. I'm afraid. I don't know what's true and what's not. I need help. Josh must listen to me!

CHAPTER **5**
THE PROOF

Josh Dial was still taking medicine each day. Dr. Penn had given him some red pills. Josh said they made him feel much better.

"Forget the pills!" Kate screamed that Wednesday night. She threw the whole bottle into the trash smasher. "Listen to me, Josh! Listen to me now! Tomorrow I have to go in for medicine again. You have to listen to me while I can still think."

"I had a baby!" Kate cried, "I know it's true. They're controlling us, Josh. It's the drugs and the mind-bending. They're making us forget our own pasts. They're making us forget our child."

Josh looked at Kate as if she'd lost her mind. He tried to calm her down.

"I remember everything, Kate," he said. "I remember our trip into the Wilds. I remember the citizen camp we stayed in and the maps we made. There's nothing wrong with my memory."

"Josh, you don't understand." Kate was crying now. "They leave us some memories, but only the ones they want us to have. The drugs and the mind-bending take care of any memories they want to destroy. Believe me, Josh, it can be done!"

Josh shook his head. He took Kate's arm and tried to pull her to him. "You're going through a rocky time, Kate," he said. "But think of what you're saying. *It just can't be true!*"

Kate pulled away and rushed down the hall to the study. With her fingernails, she began scratching at its white walls.

Josh followed her. "Stop it, Kate!" he shouted. "You don't know what you're doing."

"Look!" Kate cried. "Look at this!"

Josh went over to the wall. "What?" he asked. "Look at what?"

Kate had scratched off the paint from a small spot on the wall.

"Look!" she cried again.

Under the white paint was a light yellow color.

"It's yellow," Kate shouted. "I don't remember this room being yellow. Do you?"

Josh shook his head. "No, I don't," he said. "But what does it matter? Kate, what's gotten into you?"

"This room was yellow, Josh. I think we painted it yellow—a soft light baby's yellow! Josh, I don't remember when, but I think we painted this room for our own child."

Josh looked at Kate without saying a word.

"I have to make you understand," Kate said as she rushed out of the study. Josh sat down on the desk. He put his feet on the chair and his head in his hands.

"They're going to have to make your medicine stronger, Kate. You must stop this!" He listened to his wife banging about the apartment.

"What are you doing, Kate?" Josh called. "You're destroying us! Our life is good. We have everything we want. If you keep acting like this, we'll lose it all."

Kate came storming from their room. "Here!" she cried. "I knew if I looked hard enough I'd find something."

She sat down on the floor next to Josh's chair. She was calmer now. She had her proof.

"I pulled apart our bedroom chest of drawers," she said. "These pictures were caught way in the back. They must have fallen down behind the bottom drawer. Did you know there are slides missing from the wall-screen file? Someone must have taken them, maybe while they were here painting the study. But they missed these. Look at them!"

Kate owned a beautiful camera that was more than 50 years old. With it, she and Josh had taken some pictures, snapshots, Kate called them. There was still a little shop out on Riverside Row that could print the film.

The first picture showed Josh smiling and looking sharp in a black coat and hat. He was standing near a stream. Beside him was a wooden rocking horse.

"I don't remember this at all," Josh said. "But that rocking horse must have been made out in the Wilds. There isn't much in the Metro that's made of wood these days. But what would I be doing with a rocking horse? And Kate, this picture couldn't have been taken very long ago. I look just like I do now." He shook his head. "How can it be that I don't remember?"

Kate handed Josh the next picture. It was one of Kate. She looked beautiful and very happy standing there beside the stream and the rocking horse. She was wearing a large blue top and her hair was pulled back with a blue

bow. Kate's stomach went way out in front of her. Anyone could see that she was going to have a baby.

Kate and Josh looked at each other. Josh pulled Kate close to him. They did not remember, but they did believe what the pictures showed them.

CHAPTER **6**

A CAMP IN THE WILDS

Josh picked up his next bottle of pills, but he no longer took the drugs. He wanted to remember. At least, he decided, he could try to clear his mind.

Without the pills, he began to act like the strong and sure Josh of old.

It was not as easy for Kate. The doctor still had her coming in for her medicine three times a week. She had to take the doses that fogged her thinking.

"We must do something," Kate said. "If I'm always drugged, we'll never find our child."

Late one night she took Josh with her to the Chem Lab. She had pass cards that opened all the doors. The man watching the lab knew Kate well. She had no problem getting herself and Josh in.

Kate worked all night while Josh kept a lookout. Before morning she'd come up with something she could take to keep Dr. Penn's drugs from working.

Josh and Kate did not know if they'd ever get back their lost memories. Even so, they were both sure that they had a child somewhere.

But where was that child? And why had their baby been taken from them?

They spent long nights lying awake trying to remember. It was hard work, so hard it sometimes brought tears to Kate's eyes. But they kept at it, bringing back everything they could of the past year.

The trip into the Wilds had come about suddenly. Kate had visited Dr. Penn for a checkup. Soon after that, Josh got word of the trip. Because he was very strong and very bright, Josh was often sent on such trips. Kate had never gone with him. But this was to be a long trip. The Metro government wanted many maps. Josh would be away for months. It would be better, the government said, if Kate went also. Kate was glad to go with him.

Nearly 18 million people made their homes in the Metro. Each year a few hundred asked to leave. They wanted to try to make it on their own. Only some were given permission.

These people lived in citizen camps. They made their homes in small buildings grouped together deep in the Wilds. They had no contact with the Metro. In fact, contact was against the law. Once in a while an explorer like Josh

was sent out to map the country around the camps.

The citizen camp that Josh and Kate visited that year held only a hundred people. Kate had thought they'd be dull and strange. Instead, she found bright happy men and women. Their children laughed and played, and no one seemed to care what was going on in the Metro.

"They don't wear rating cards," Kate had said to Josh. She pointed to the 20-A card pinned to her shirt. "How do we know how smart and how strong they are? How do *they* know?"

"It doesn't seem to matter to them," Josh had said.

Kate and Josh moved into a little house at one end of the camp. They would live there while they made day trips to map the nearby lands.

Soon they met a young man and woman named John and Meg. The two campers had lived their whole lives in the Wilds.

"John's parents came here long ago," Meg said. "And so did mine. We were both born in this camp. We'd never think of leaving. Our lives are here where no fog hides the sky. There's one to control the cold or the rain or the snow. And there's no one to control us either."

Kate had wondered why anyone would want to leave the Metro. Life there was easy. Everyone had a job, enough food to eat, and time for fun. In the citizen camp the days were full of hard work.

"You might not understand," Meg had said, "but I'll try to explain it. My mother was fat. She didn't want to take weight-control drugs. The Metro doctors said she had to. They said no one could be fat. They said that too much weight could make a person sick and that it was ugly. They forced my mother to take the drugs. They said she'd lose her job, her apartment, everything, if she didn't. It was then that my parents saw how little control they had over their own lives. So they asked to leave. It was five years before they were told they could."

Kate remembered Meg's story. She remembered Meg's round face and John's hearty laugh. She remembered helping Josh draw up maps. But she could not remember anything about a pregnancy. Only the snapshots said there'd ever been one.

"I wish we could contact John and Meg," Kate said. "They'd remember us. And they'd know about the baby."

"There's no way to reach them," Josh said. "It would mean a long trip by road car. Your doctor would never let us go."

Kate looked deep into Josh's eyes. "They've erased a part of our past," she said. "With drugs and mind-bending, they've made it seem like some things never happened."

"But they *did* happen," Josh said. "We were sent on the trip to hide your pregnancy. No one here knows anything about it. I think that was all planned out."

"Why?" Kate asked. "There are so many babies. What do they want with our child?"

As they thought about it, it became clearer. Josh and Kate were special. There were not many 20-A's, maybe 2,000 in the whole Metro. Two 20-A's were more likely than others to have a 20-A child. The Metro government wanted these children for themselves. They wanted to bring them up in youth camps and fill them with the right ideas. A 20-A who worked for the government and had the right ideas was of great value. A 20-A with the wrong ideas about things could be a danger.

"Look at us," Josh said. "We grew up in a youth camp. The government placed us in jobs as soon as we left it. We didn't question the experts. We did what we were told. We believed what they said about our parents. When we married, it was probably part of their grand plan. Our minds and our bodies have always belonged to the Metro."

"But not our baby," Kate said. "They won't have our baby."

CHAPTER **7**

A SECRET FILE

"Hello. Dr. Penn? I'm not feeling well today. I think I need to come in to see you. Can you fit me in this afternoon? I don't mind waiting in your office if you could give me just a few minutes."

Kate watched Dr. Penn's face on the telephone screen. She tried to keep her own face calm. She didn't want to give Dr. Penn any reason to think something strange was going on. Kate hoped to find time in the doctor's office alone. She had to get into Dr. Penn's records. Perhaps something there would lead her to her baby.

"Of course, Kate," Dr. Penn said, "I can always make time for you. I'll see you around 3:00."

Kate was in Dr. Penn's office only a few minutes when the doctor was called away.

A loud voice came over the doctor's speaker box. "Problem in 103-R!"

"I'll be back as soon as I can, Kate," Dr. Penn said. "I'm sorry, but it's hard to plan for these last minute office calls." Dr. Penn hurried off to the 103rd floor of the hospital.

Kate did not wait a minute. She had to take a chance. She went to the doctor's computer screen and called up Dr. Penn's files. She hit the keys quickly until records for the month of May were before her.

The file said Kate Dial had come in for a stomach operation and was later sent home. The words on the screen backed up everything the doctor had told Kate. Kate was disappointed. She was about to turn the computer off when a strange note flashed on the screen.

"See hard copy," it said. "Hard copy?" Kate didn't understand. Hard copy was paper. No one had kept records on paper for years. But somewhere, Kate decided, there must be a real piece of paper that could tell her about her child.

Kate turned off the screen. She felt as if she'd come to a dead end. Where in the world could she look for one little piece of paper? Records on computers were one thing. There were many ways to get into computer files. It really was just a matter of knowing the right buttons to press. But a piece of paper? Kate had no idea where to start hunting.

She looked around the office. There weren't any file cabinets or locked drawers.

When Dr. Penn returned, Kate told her she'd been having bad headaches. The doctor looked Kate over, found nothing wrong, and gave her some yellow pills.

"It looks like you're doing just fine, Kate. These pills should take care of any headaches."

Kate thanked the doctor and turned to go.

"By the way, Kate," Dr. Penn said, "we're pleased that you've been coming in on time for your medicine." The doctor had no idea Kate's own chemicals were fighting the hospital drugs. "In another two or three weeks we should be able to cut back on your doses. Soon you'll be back to your old life. Everything will be just as it was before the operation."

Kate forced a smile, thanked Dr. Penn, and left the office.

Now Kate and Josh had a new problem. How could they find the paper they needed?

Secretly, they talked to people at the hospital. They questioned those who would not know them. They talked to the kitchen help and to the people who cleaned the halls. Many of the jobs could have been done by robots. But people needed work. The Metro had to find jobs for those with lower ratings.

The man who swept the halls on the hospital's lower floors was a friendly worker named Dave. Dave loved to talk. He was rated only 4-G, but he knew things about that hospital that few others knew. Kate won him over with a smile and a box of orange candies.

From Dave, Kate and Josh learned about a room on the lowest floor of the hospital. There were files there, Dave said, paper files.

"They're from long, long ago. No one uses them now. I've only swept that room a few times. I don't like it down there. It's where they take the ones that don't make it. They freeze some of them, you know. And later they cut them up to find out what went wrong." Dave shook as if he were cold himself. "The room with the papers is way in the back, behind where they keep the cold, stiff bodies. I never see anyone go in there."

"Take us there," Josh said.

Dave was afraid. It could mean his job.

Josh and Kate begged Dave to help them. They promised him presents and money. They told him how important he was and how much they needed him as a friend. The 4-G looked at the 20-A cards pinned to Josh's and Kate's coats. It would really be something if he could call two 20-A's his friends.

"Okay," Dave finally said. He took the money that Josh handed him. It was more than Dave had ever seen at one time. "But no one had better catch us!"

It was very cool in the underground hallway.

"That's where they keep the bodies," Dave whispered as he pointed. "We have to go through that room to the one in back of it."

They walked up to a wide door. Josh pushed on the door, but it didn't move. "They keep it locked," Dave said. He took a folder out of his pocket. In it were many key-cards. He pulled one out and slipped it into the door. Then he pushed the door open.

The room was dim and very cold. One wall was lined with big metal doors. Cooling machines made a soft noise.

"Behind those doors on the walls," Dave said. "That's where they keep the ones that don't make it."

He led them across the room to a wooden door at the far end.

"This is it," Dave said. "But it's locked too."

"Do you have the key-card?" Josh asked.

"This part of the hospital is real old," Dave said. "The door's made of wood. Key-cards don't work on this kind of door." He pointed to a strange hole in the door. "It takes a special key," Dave went on. "A key that's long and made of metal. I don't have one."

"What will we do?" Kate asked.

Dave smiled. His eyes were bright below his orange hair. "I know some things you smart people don't," he said. He pulled a metal tool from his pocket and held it up for Josh and Kate to look at. "It's called a screwdriver," he said. "You ever see one?"

Josh and Kate both shook their heads. They never fixed things that broke. Robots or other people did that for them.

Dave put the end of the screwdriver into the hole in the door. He turned it until he heard a click. Dave pushed on the door. It opened.

Dave reached in, turned on a light, and stepped inside. Kate and Josh followed him. The room was small and dusty and filled with file cabinets. Each cabinet was marked to show the dates on the files it held. The files went from 2085 clear back to the 1980's.

"I'm leaving," Dave said. "You're nice people, but I don't want to lose my job." He turned and hurried out.

Kate and Josh circled the room. The dust on the cabinets was so thick that Kate began to sneeze.

"Now where would they have hidden that file?" Josh said.

"There's so much dust!" Kate said as she sneezed.

"The dust!" Josh said. "That's our clue."

He began looking more closely at each cabinet. "Here it is!" he said, pointing to one of them.

"How do you know?" Kate asked. "There are so many."

Josh ran his finger along the place where the drawer fit into the cabinet. "The dust isn't as thick here. This cabinet's been opened, and not too long ago. Someone's been in it."

Josh pulled open the drawer. It was filled with file folders. All but a few of them looked yellow with age. "We've got it!" he said.

In one of the newer-looking folders Josh found the records they needed.

The records showed that Kate Dial had given birth to a baby boy on May 9, 2085. He had rated high on all the tests. As the child of 20-A's, he was the valuable property of the Metro. The child was sent to Youth Camp Blackberry on the day he was born.

CHAPTER **8**

YOUTH CAMP BLACKBERRY

For the next few days Kate and Josh acted as if nothing had changed. They worked hard and visited with friends. And they spent all the rest of their time planning. They were going to get their baby back.

On July 9, 2085, Kate's and Josh's baby was two months old. It was a Tuesday, a work day. No one thought it strange when someone from the Metro Chem Lab showed up to visit the youth camp.

"I'm here to do blood testing," Kate said. "We have a new problem showing up in some of the children." Kate carried a blue bag. Her Chem Lab I.D. card was pinned to her blue lab coat.

Josh waited in the car on a dirt path near the fence. He was sitting in a road car, one with big heavy tires and its own power-packed engine. The car belonged to the Metro

Transport Department. It was brand new and was not like his own computer-run car. The road car could leave the Metro. It did not need to get its power from the transport lines.

Inside the youth camp, no one took much note of Kate. They had no reason to guess that she was up to something. She was free to move about as she pleased.

Babies up to three months old were kept on the third floor of Building White. As Kate stepped out of the elevator she heard the crying of many babies. One of them, she was sure, was hers.

A woman dressed in red with long red hair sat behind a desk. Other men and women, the nurses, moved among the beds. They all had red, blue, or yellow hair and clothes.

"Bright colors keep the babies interested and happy," the red-haired woman told Kate. She saw Kate's I.D. card and let her have free run of the floor. She asked no questions as Kate began taking drops of blood from the babies' toes.

A half hour passed. Kate had to make her move soon. But she still had no idea which baby was hers.

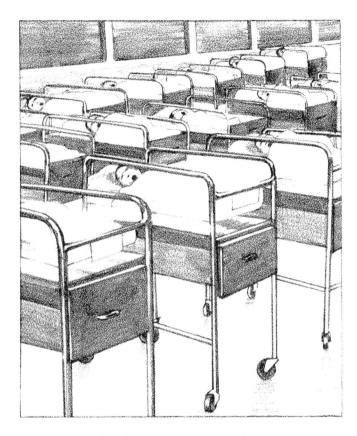

She went back to the front desk.

"Your job here must be very hard," Kate said to the woman there. "How in the world do you keep track of all these babies? How do you even know how old each one is?"

The woman was pleased by Kate's show of interest. She saw that Kate was a 20-A. She was a 12-L. She was glad to be Kate's friend.

She pushed the keys of her computer and showed Kate that there was a file on each child. The babies had all been given names and ratings. Their birthdays had been recorded, but there was no record of their parents.

"See here," the woman said. "The little girl in bed 16, row 21, is Bev Cup. Bev was born just last month at Metro Caring Hospital. She's an 18-B. We have some smart little babies here." The woman spoke as if it were all her own doing.

"It's just wonderful how you keep track of all this," Kate said. "Can you tell all kinds of things about the babies? Can you even tell how many babies have come in on a given day?"

"Of course," the woman said with a wide smile. "Just pick a day, any day."

Kate's heart was pounding. She knew she was close to finding her own child.

She kept her voice very calm. "Oh, let's see," Kate said. "Today's the 9th. How about the 9th two months ago?"

"May 9th," the woman said as she pressed some keys. A list showed on the screen. Kate looked over it quickly while the woman talked on. She needed a listing for a boy born in Metro Hospital of Hope.

There it was! Web Tab, they had named him. A silly name, Kate thought. Web Tab, rated 20-A. Her baby was just across the room, in bed 42, row 17. Kate checked the list again. No other baby boy had come in from Metro Hospital of Hope on May 9.

Kate left the front desk and went back to her blood testing. She tried to stay calm. As she worked her way toward row 17, she smiled at all the nurses.

And then she was there, standing over bed 42, looking into the bluest little eyes.

"My baby," Kate whispered. "My boy."

CHAPTER 9
THE THEFT

Kate knew it was time. She'd been on the new-baby floor for too long. The nurses would begin to wonder.

Kate lifted the tiny baby in bed 42 and walked toward the desk.

Some of the nurses looked at Kate strangely as she crossed the room with little Web Tab. Kate met their eyes. They did not say anything.

Kate spoke to the red-haired woman. "It looks like there might be a little problem with this child," she said. "I'm taking him down for more testing. We don't want him passing anything on to the other children."

The woman looked surprised. She didn't want to question Kate. But there were rules about letting babies leave the floor.

Kate didn't wait for the woman's okay. She moved on quickly, holding the baby tight.

The woman in red stood up. She wanted someone to help her decide what to do. The other nurses watched wide-eyed.

"Wait!" The red-haired woman finally shouted. "You can't just take that baby!"

But it was too late. Kate was already on the fire stairs. She'd known the elevator could be stopped and that she might be trapped on it. So she'd decided to run down the three flights.

As she came through a door to the outside, she saw men running toward the building. They had to be after her.

Kate raced across the grounds holding her baby. He was crying now.

"Don't you worry," Kate said as she ran. "We'll all be safe soon."

There had never been a kidnapping at Youth Camp Blackberry. Metro citizens were well controlled with drugs and the lessons they'd learned as children. The law was the law. No one had ever caused any trouble there.

A loud sharp voice came over a speaker. It could be heard all across the grounds, ordering that Kate be stopped.

They'd be waiting at the gates. Kate knew that. She headed for the fence that circled the camp.

Josh had left the car and hidden behind a tree on the other side of the fence. As he saw Kate coming, he rushed forward to meet her. Kate lifted the baby over to him and then climbed the fence. They ran for the car and jumped in through its open hatch.

"Josh Dial," Kate said, "meet your son!"

Josh couldn't speak. He touched the baby's face and his little hands.

"He's ours, Kate, isn't he? He's really ours?"

Kate smiled. She closed her eyes and hoped her heart would stop pounding. She then took the baby from Josh.

"Hurry now," she said.

Josh pressed some buttons and set the road car's controls for top speed. The great engine roared as the car pulled out of its hiding place.

Kate, Josh, and their son were in danger as long as they were in the Metro. Their big road car was too easy to spot among the little bubble topped metro-transports. If they were going to be safe they had to get out.

CHAPTER **10**

A NEW DAY

Word of the kidnapping at Youth Camp Blackberry reached Metro Hospital of Hope. Dr. Penn walked the floor of her office. She ran her hands through her short green hair and shouted.

"Get on it!" she cried. "Get the speed-cars out after them. Call up the air-darters. We can spot them quicker from the sky. I want that 20–A baby back where he belongs."

Dr. Penn fell into her chair. Then she jumped up again and began walking up and down. "I should have seen it coming," she said out loud. "How could I have been tricked by that woman?" Suddenly Dr. Penn stood still. Her face turned white. She reached over and pressed a button on her speaker box.

"This is Dr. Penn," she shouted. "Don't let a word of this get out. The citizens must not learn of acts against the Metro. Such things just do not happen!"

Kate was not surprised when an air-darter buzzed overhead. The little plane was flying below the fog bank so that the pilot could spot them.

"Josh, I'm sure he's seen us."

"Don't worry, Kate. He can't land here. All he can do is report in. They'll probably send cars out after us, but I can outrun any of them."

It wasn't long before the speed-cars showed up. Like Josh's road car, the speed-cars had big engines of their own. They were free of the transport lines.

There was a chase. It was just like the old-time car chases Kate sometimes saw on the wall-screen.

Citizens watched wide-eyed and didn't know what to think. This was far from an everyday sight in the orderly Metro.

The speed-cars were fast, but they didn't stand a chance. The tires on Josh's car were wide and thick. They could take the car almost anyplace. Josh didn't need to look for a road in order to find a shortcut.

Kate and Josh were nearly to the edge of the Metro when they were forced to stop. They were blocked in by speed-cars in front of them and buildings on both sides.

Kate was scared. There wasn't enough room to turn the car around. She held her baby close.

"Josh! They have us. They'll take him away!"

But Kate didn't know everything that the new car could do. Josh pushed a button. The body of the road car lifted above its tires and turned around in a half-circle. In seconds they were speeding the other way.

Kate and Josh made it out of the Metro. Dirt roads took them into the countryside. Soon, even those roads came to an end. There was no need for roads this far out. Who would want to come out here?

Josh and Kate headed for the citizen camp they had visited earlier that year.

Kate looked behind her. She could no longer see the tall buildings. She could only see what looked like a big ball of fog.

"John and Meg will help us find a place to hide," Josh said.

Kate smiled. "It's summer," she said. "It's really summer out here. Stop the car, Josh, just for a minute. They'll never find us in the Wilds. No one knows the land as well as you do. Please, I just want to stop and feel the air."

"Just for a minute," Josh said. "We have to get to the camp."

Outside the car, Kate let the warm wind blow in her face. She held her baby up to the sun.

"We'll be safe now," Josh said. "They may look for us for a while, but they'll give up. They won't want to let the news of our escape leak out."

"But you know, Kate," he went on. "We have nothing now, nothing but each other and our son. We can never, never, go back. Life is going to change. It may be hard. We won't have a fine apartment above the clouds or a wall-screen or robots."

"And no little red pills," Kate said. "No Luradine and no one controlling our lives."

"Come on," Josh said. "We have to be on our way."

Kate got back in the car with the baby. Josh started the engine. Then, before setting off, he turned to Kate and his son. The baby looked at his father with big blue eyes. He waved his little hands and started crying.

"Yes, young man," Josh said. "Your mom heard you crying. She heard you crying, and so we came to get you."

Kate pulled the 20-A card from her baby's blanket. Then she took off her own card and leaned over and took Josh's. She threw them out her window. Josh hit a button. As Josh, Kate, and their baby roared off, their cards blew away in the dust.